LEGAL TERMINOLOGY AND PHRASES

Master 350+ Essential Business, Enterprise, Commercial and Investment Terms And Phrases Explained With Examples In 10 Minutes A Day

DR. PETER JOHNSON

Copyright © 2018

All rights reserved.

ISBN: 9781726789684

TEXT COPYRIGHT © DR. PETER JOHNSON

All rights reserved. No part of this guide may be reproduced in any form without permission in writing from the publisher, except for brief quotations used for publishable articles or reviews.

Legal Disclaimer

The information contained in this book and its contents is not designed to replace any form of medical or professional advice; and is not meant to replace the need for independent medical, financial, legal, or other professional advice or services that may be required. The content and information in this book have been provided for educational and entertainment purposes only.

The content and information contained in this book have been compiled from sources deemed reliable, and they are accurate to the best of the Author's knowledge, information, and belief. However, the Author cannot guarantee its accuracy and validity and therefore cannot be held liable for any errors and/or omissions. Further, changes are periodically made to this book as needed. Where appropriate and/or necessary, you must consult a professional (including but not limited to your doctor, attorney, financial advisor, or other such professional) before using any of the suggested remedies, techniques, and/or information in this book.

Upon using this book's contents and information, you agree to hold harmless the Author from any damages, costs, and expenses, including any legal fees potentially resulting from the application of any of the information in this book. This disclaimer applies to any loss, damages, or injury caused by the use and application of this book's contents, whether directly or indirectly, whether for breach of contract, tort, negligence, personal injury, criminal intent, or under any other circumstance.

You agree to accept all risks of using the information presented in this book.

You agree that by continuing to read this book, where appropriate and/or necessary, you shall consult a professional (including but not limited to your doctor, attorney, financial advisor, or other such professional) before using any of the suggested remedies, techniques, or information in this book.

Table of Contents

INTRODUCTION 6

SECTION A: 8

SECTION B: 12

SECTION C: 17

SECTION D: 25

SECTION E: 29

SECTION F: 33

SECTION G: 37

SECTION H: 38

SECTION I: 39

SECTION J: 42

SECTION L: 43

SECTION M: 46

SECTION N: 48

SECTION O: 49

SECTION P: 52

SECTION R: 56

SECTION S: 60

SECTION T: 67

SECTION U: 70

SECTION V: 71

SECTION W: 72

CONCLUSION 73

CHECK OUT OTHER BOOKS 75

INTRODUCTION

Thank you and congratulate you for downloading the book *"Legal Terminology And Phrases: Master 350+ Essential Business, Enterprise, Commercial and Investment Terms And Phrases Explained With Examples In 10 Minutes A Day."*

With a clear, concise, and engaging writing style, Dr. Peter Johnson will help you with a practical understanding of legal topics about *Business, Enterprise, Commercial, Investment, Securities, and Real Estate Trading* **and much much more.** This book delivers extensive coverage of every aspect of the law and details the duties a paralegal is expected to perform when working within business law. High-level, comprehensive coverage is combined with cutting-edge developments and foundational concepts. If you'd like to increase your wide range of legal vocabulary as well as enhance your knowledge of *Business, Enterprise, Commercial, Investment, Securities, and Real Estate Trading* laws, then this book may be the most important book that you will ever read.

As the author of the book, I promise this book will be an invaluable source of legal reference for professionals, international lawyers, law students, business professionals and anyone else who want to improve their use of legal terminology, succinct clarification of legal terms and have a better understanding of laws on *Business, Enterprise, Commercial, Investment, Securities, and Real Estate Trading*. This book provides you with a comprehensive and highly practical approach in legal contexts, the world of business, all substantive and procedural aspects of business law. All legal terms and phrases are well written and explained clearly in plain English.

Thank you again for purchasing this book, and I hope you enjoy it.

Let's get started!

SECTION A:

Authorization: an official permission is given to someone to do something.

Performance of a task without authorization.

The authorization must be made in writing, unless being agreed.

The authorization of representatives to attend the General Meeting of Shareholders must be made in writing using the form provided by the company.

A due debt: a debt that has not been paid at a particular time.

The Director or General Director must not increase salaries or pay bonuses if the company is not able to pay due debts.

When the company fails to pay the due debts and other liabilities, the company's owner must not receive profit.

Right after the dividend is fully paid, the company is still able to pay due debts and other liabilities.

A service contract: an agreement between a contractor and customer for maintaining and repairing a product over a specified period.

Rights and obligations of parties to service contracts.

A service contract shall be expressed in written form or verbal.

Sale promotion service contracts.

Commercial advertising service contracts.

Auction: a public sale in which goods or property are sold to the person who offers the highest price.

Auction of goods.

To organize auctions.

Auction participants are organizations and individuals that register to participate in auctions.

The auctioneer: a person who is in charge of/manages/ conducts an auction.

An auction shall be conducted in the following order:

1. The auctioneer makes a roll call of registered participants in the goods auction;

2. The auctioneer presents each auctioned goods item, repeats their reserve prices, answer questions of the auction participants, and ask them to offer bids;

Anti-competitive: intended to compete against each other unfairly, especially in business

Anti-competitive effects.

Anti-competitive agreement.

Enterprises intending to enter into anti-competitive agreements shall submit an application for exemption for prohibited anti-competitive agreements to the National Competition Commission.

Agency contract: a contract expressing that a business or organization represents, acts on behalf of another business, or person.

Unless otherwise agreed, principals shall have the following rights:

1. To request agents to make payments or deliver goods under agency contracts;

2. To inspect and supervise the performance of contracts by agents;

A trade secret: a formula, process, information, commercial method that is known, used, and kept secret by a particular company.

Trade secret infringement in the following forms:

a) Assessing and acquiring trade secrets by going against security measures of the owner of such trade secrets;

b) Disclosing or using trade secrets without the consent of the owner.

Acquisition: the process of buying something in some other way.

The acquisition is prohibited if the acquirer has more than 50% of the market share after the acquisition.

Assistance funds: an amount of money that can be used for purposes to be decided later.

Investors may access and make use of loan capital, assistance funds, land, and other resources as prescribed by law.

Amendment: the process of making changes to a law or document.

Rules for making amendments to the company's charter.

Assistance funds: an amount of money that can be used for purposes to be decided later.

Investors may access and make use of loan capital, assistance funds, land, and other resources as prescribed by law.

Assessment: the act of evaluating or estimating of the nature, or quality of something.

Assessment services: Assessment services are commercial activities whereby traders perform necessary jobs to determine actual conditions of goods, results of the provision of services and other contents at the request of customers.

A bailee: a person or party who has been entrusted with the custody of a piece of property, without transfer of ownership.

In cases where the leased goods are received by a bailee other than a carrier for delivery, risks shall be passed to the lessee as soon as the bailee acknowledge the lessee's right to possess the leased goods;

SECTION B:

Business means the continuous activity of a particular company that manufactures, sells products or services on the market to earn profit.

Obligations of enterprises: Declare, pay taxes and fulfill other financial obligation as prescribed by law.

Names of branches, representative offices, and business locations.

Business location means a place where the enterprise does particular business activities.

Business operation: refers to the operation of a company with the intention of earning revenue.

The Director of a company is the person who administers the everyday business operation of the company and is responsible to the Board of members for the performance of his/her rights and obligations.

The company's owner has the rights to supervise and assess the company's business operation;

Business line: a particular kind of merchandise or product.

Enterprises have the right to engage in the business lines that are not prohibited by law.

The enterprise shall be granted the Certificate of Business registration when the registered business lines are not banned;

Business efficiency: how much output a business produces.

This software enables us to get the very best solution to improve our business efficiency.

The Board of members

Minutes of meetings of the Board of members.

The Board of Directors: a group of people who are elected to represent the shareholders' interests.

The Board of Directors shall supervise and urge shareholders to pay for the registered shares fully and punctually.

Meetings of the Board of Directors:

The Board of Directors may hold periodic and extraordinary meetings. The Board of Directors shall hold meetings at the company's headquarter or other locations.

Bankruptcy: the state of being bankrupt.

The company's owner has the rights to:

a) Decide the company's restructuring, dissolution, and petition for bankruptcy;

b) Withdraw the entire value of the company's asset value after the dissolution or bankruptcy process is completed;

Branch: a location where business is conducted.

Representative office: a business office that is established by a company in a foreign country.

Establishment of branches, representative offices.

Names of representative offices, branches, and business locations.

Be liable for: to be legally responsible for something.

Members of limited liability company are liable for debts and other liabilities of the enterprise up to the value of capital they contribute to the enterprise.

The company's owner of a single-member limited liability company is liable for the company's debts and other liabilities up to the company's charter capital.

Business opportunities: involves the sale or lease of any product, or service.

Responsibilities of Controllers:

Act in the best interest of the company and its shareholders; do not use information, secrets, business opportunities of the company;

Bond issuance: the act of issuing (supplying or distributing) bonds.

Convertible bonds: a type of bond that gives the bondholder the right to convert it into a specified number of shares of common stock in the issuing company.

A joint-stock company is entitled to issue convertible bonds.

Business investment: the money spent on creating, developing, or improving a business with the expectations of future returns.

Disputes over business investments shall be settled through negotiation and conciliation.

Business cooperation contract: a cooperation agreement between two companies to carry out specific business activities for mutual benefit.

Making investments under business cooperation contracts.

Execute a business cooperation contract overseas;

Business organization: an entity aimed at carrying on a commercial enterprise to provide services, products or both, to meet the needs of the customers.

Investments made by foreign-invested business organizations.

Business organizations are organizations that make business investments.

Broker: someone who buys and sells goods or assets for others or arranges transactions between a seller and a buyer for a commission when the deal is executed.

Unless otherwise agreed, a commercial broker shall have the following obligations:

1. To preserve samples of goods and documents assigned for the performance of brokerage activities, and to return them to the principals after the completion of brokerage;

2. Not to disclose or supply information to the detriment of the interests of the principals;

Brokerage: the act of buying and selling goods or assets for others.

Bidding: the offering of a particular amount of money for something, especially at an auction.

Bidding for goods or services.

Bidder: someone who offers a particular amount of money for something, especially at an auction.

Bid solicitors shall have to provide bidders with instructions on the tendering conditions, procedures to be applied in the bidding process, and to answer questions of bidders.

Bidders shall not be allowed to receive back their bid deposits or collaterals in cases where they withdraw bid dossiers after the expiration of the time limit for submitting bid dossiers (referred to as "bidding closure"), fail to enter into contracts or refuse to perform contracts in cases where they are bid winners.

Bid opening: Bids are normally opened in a public.

Bidders are not allowed to amend their bid dossiers after the bid opening.

The time of bid opening shall be the time immediately after the bidding closure.

Date, time and place of the bid opening;

Building sale: the selling of a building.

Building sale agreement.

The selling of a building must associate with the piece of land.

Building lease: a lease of a building for a certain period of time.

The lessor may unilaterally terminate performance of building lease agreement if the lessee intentionally cause serious damage to the leased building;

SECTION C:

Charter capital means the total value of assets that are contributed or promised to be contributed by members/partners in a certain period and stated in the charter of the company.

The company may increase its charter capital when:

a) Capital contributions are made by new members;

b) Capital contribution of members is increased.

Charter capital of a limited liability company is the total value of the capital contribution to the company promised by the members.

Certificate of Business registration means a paper or electronic file issued to an enterprise which contains information about business registration.

Capital contribution means the contribution of an amount of money or assets to establish a new enterprise.

The capital contribution shall be recorded in writing if asset ownership registration is not mandatory.

Capital contribution to company establishment.

Company member means any person who holds the shares of a company.

After all debts and dissolution costs are paid, the remaining value shall be received by the company members according to their holding of stakes or shares in the company.

Competitiveness: the ability of a business to compete.

Increasing the competitiveness of local enterprises on the international market;

Contributed assets: assets that are owned by the contributing entity.

Assessing contributed assets.

Determining accurate values of contributed assets.

Transfer of ownership of contributed assets.

Convertible: able to be changed in function or form.

Convertible foreign currencies.

A joint-stock company is entitled to issue convertible bonds.

Chief accountant: the head accountant in the accounts department of a large organization.

The Board of members has the following rights:

a) Decide the increase or decrease of charter capital;

b) Decide the salaries, bonuses, and other benefits for the Chairperson of the Board of members, Director/General Director, Chief Accountant, and other managers.

Chief Executive Officer = the company's President: the main person who is responsible for managing a company.

The Chief Executive Officer is designated by the owner.

On behalf of the company's owner, the company's President shall perform the rights and obligations of the company.

The company's bank account.

Extraordinary information must be disclosed on the company's website of any of the events below:

a) The company's bank account is frozen or unfrozen;

b) Part of or all of the business operation is suspended; the Certificate of Business registration is revoked;

Corporate amalgamation: a process in which two corporations join and become a large one.

Two or some companies may consolidate into a new company.

Consolidation: the action or process of combining two or more corporations into a single new corporation.

If the consolidated company has more than 50% of the market share after consolidation, consolidation is prohibited.

Consolidating companies

Consolidated company

Consolidation contract

Certificate of investment registration: a paper or electronic document containing the registered information about the investment project of the investor.

The Certificate of investment registration is required in the following case:

Investment projects of foreign investors;

When the Certificate of investment registration has to be adjusted, the investor shall follow the procedures for adjusting the Certificate of investment registration.

Capital: a large sum of money or property that you use to start a business.

Making investment by buying capital contributions of business organizations.

Investors are entitled to buy capital contributions of business organizations.

Conditional business lines: the business lines in which the investment must satisfy certain conditions for reasons of social order and security, national defense and security, public health or social ethics.

The conditional business lines shall be posted on the National Company Registration Portal.

Clean energy: renewable energy (wind energy, solar energy, hydro energy).

Renewable energy: energy from a source that is produced by wind, sun, and other sources that will never be depleted.

Cultivation: the act or process of cultivating something.

Business lines that are given investment incentives:

a) Production of new materials, new energy, clean energy, renewable energy; productions of products with at least 30% value added; energy-saving products;

b) Cultivation, processing of agriculture products, forestry products, aquaculture products;

Competition: the activity of competing (the process of trying to get or win something).

Competition legal proceedings

Unfair competition practices

Freedom of competition in business

Commercial activities: any particular transaction or other activities undertaken as part of a commercial enterprise.

Traders are entitled to conduct commercial activities in occupations and sectors which are not banned by law.

Commercial: relating to the act of buying and selling of goods.

Commercial promotion means activities of promoting, including sale promotion, display and exhibition of goods and services, commercial advertisement, etc.

Obligations of representative offices:

1. To conduct commercial promotion activities within the scope permitted by this Law.

2. To pay taxes, fees and charges, and fulfil other financial obligations provided for by law.

Commercial advertising means commercial promotion activities of traders aimed at introducing to customers their goods and service business activities.

Commercial contract: a legally binding agreement between parties in business.

Rights and obligations in commercial contracts.

Commercial practices mean any act directly connected with the promotion, including advertising, and marketing.

Application of international commercial practices, treaties, and foreign laws.

Parties to commercial transactions may agree to apply international commercial practices or foreign laws.

Commercial intermediary activities: activities such as representation for traders, commercial brokerage, and commercial agency.

Commercial association: a company aimed at promoting the commercial interests of an area.

Commercial associations

The establishment of commercial associations is to protect the legitimate rights and interests of traders.

Commercial brokerage

Commercial brokerage means a commercial activity whereby a trader acts as an intermediary (referred to as broker) between parties selling and purchasing goods and shall be entitled to a remuneration under a brokerage contract.

Commercial advertising: a type of advertising that is typically aimed at selling a product or service.

Conduct commercial advertising activities.

Provision of commercial advertising services.

Means of commercial advertising.

Commercial advertising products: television, radio, newspapers, and the internet that reach a large audience.

Traders shall have the right to register for protection of their intellectual property rights over commercial advertising products.

Commercial advertising products consist of information in images, actions, voices, sounds, scripts, symbols, colors and lights.

Commercial advertising service contracts

Commercial advertising service contracts must be made in writing or in other forms of equivalent legal validity.

To inspect and supervise the performance of commercial advertising service contracts.

Commercial agency: the agent who represents, acts on behalf of another individual or a business or organization.

The ownership right in commercial agency

The principal is the owner of goods or money delivered to the agent(s).

Confidentiality: the state of keeping something secret or private.

Confidentiality of bidding information.

Contract performance security.

Contract performance security measures shall be effective up to the time of completion of contractual obligations by bid winners.

Commercial assessment services: Traders providing commercial assessment services shall be allowed to provide assessment services in domains of assessment only when they fully satisfy the conditions provided by laws.

Commercial franchise: a type of license granted by a company to an individual or group enabling them to access to the franchiser's processes, and trademarks to sell a product or provide a service under the business's name.

Commercial franchise contracts must be made in writing or in other forms of equivalent legal validity.

Unless otherwise agreed, franchisees shall have the following obligations:

1. To pay franchise sums and other amounts under commercial franchise contracts;

2. To keep secret the franchised business know-how even after the expiration or termination of commercial franchise contracts;

Conciliation: the action of mediating between two disputing people or groups by mutual and friendly agreement with a view to avoiding litigation.

Conciliation between the parties by a body, organization or individual selected by the parties to act as the conciliation mediator.

Commission: a fee paid to an agent for performing a service

Real estate brokerage commission.

The real estate brokerage commission shall be agreed by contracting parties.

Closed fund means a public fund whose certificates, which have undergone a public offering, should not be bought back at the request of investors.

Closed fund certificates are issued to the fund's existing investors only by means of distribution of the right to buy transferrable closed fund certificates.

SECTION D:

Dissolution: the termination or cancellation of a corporation's existence.

Procedures for dissolution and asset liquidation of an enterprise.

Restructuring or dissolution of the company.

The decision on dissolution must contain reasons for dissolution.

The decision on dissolution shall be enclosed with the debt settlement plan and sent to the creditors.

Dividend: a payment made by a joint-stock company to its shareholders after all financial obligations are fulfilled.

Dividends may be paid in cash.

The dividend must be fully paid within 06 months from the end of the Annual General Meeting of shareholders.

Withdrawal of payment for repurchased shares or dividends.

Dissolution: the process of officially ending the existence of an organization.

Restructuring or dissolution of the company.

The company's owner has the rights to decide the company's restructuring, dissolution, and petition for bankruptcy;

Director: someone who is in charge of all or part of a company, or organization.

General Director: a person who is in charge of a large organization.

Deputy Director: someone who acts on behalf of the director.

Deputy General Director: someone who acts on behalf of the general director.

The quantity of Deputy Director/Deputy General Director shall be specified in the company's charter.

A company shall have one or some Deputy General Director/Deputy General Director.

Rights and obligations of the Deputy Director/Deputy General Director shall be specified in the company's charter or employment contract.

To redeem: to repurchase.

Redeemable preferred shares are shares that will be redeemed by the company at the request of their holders or under the conditions written thereon.

Dividend payment: a payment made by a corporation to its shareholders as a dividend.

It is permissible to make dividend payment by checks, wire transfer, or payment order by post to the shareholders' permanent residences or mailing addresses.

Domestic goods/services: goods/services that are produced or made within a particular country as apart from other countries.

Investors are not required by the State to satisfy the following requirement:

Give priority to buying, using domestic goods/services;

Delivery of goods: the process of transporting goods to a destination.

Place of delivery of goods.

Time limit for delivery of goods.

Delivery of goods before the agreed time.

Defect of the goods: a shortcoming, fault or problem that spoils the goods.

Before the time of passing the risk to the purchaser, the seller shall be liable for any defect of the goods which already exists.

If the purchaser, at the time the contract is entered into, knew or should have known any defect of the goods, the seller shall not be liable for such defect;

Determination of prices: the act of determining the prices of something.

Display and introduction of goods and services

Display and introduction of goods and services mean commercial promotion activities of traders that use goods and/or services and documents thereon to introduce such goods and/or services to customers.

Forms of display and introduction of goods and services

1. Opening showrooms for displaying and introducing goods and/or services.

2. Displaying and introducing goods and/or services at trade centers or in entertainment, sport, cultural or artistic activities.

Dispute: a disagreement, argument, or debate between people or groups.

Resolution of commercial disputes

Procedures for resolution of commercial disputes by arbitration or a court shall comply with procedures applicable to arbitrations or courts provided for by law.

Distrain: to seize someone's property to obtain payment of money owed.

The building is distrained.

Types of land that are allowed to be put on the market:

a) The land is not distrained;

b) There is no dispute about the land.

Distribution of securities

The issuing organization shall complete the distribution of securities within ninety days after the certificate of a public offering of securities becomes effective.

SECTION E:

Establishment: the act of creating or starting something such as an organization.

The establishment and operation of the enterprise.

Members shall unanimously assess the assets contributed upon the enterprise establishment.

The enterprise shall submit an application for establishment of the branch/representative office to a competent business registration authority when establishing a branch/representative office.

Economic sectors: large groups of the economy based on particular products or services.

The State ensures the legal equality of enterprises regardless of their forms and economic sectors; and acknowledges the legitimate profitability of the business.

Enterprise means a company or business that has its own name, assets, and office.

Owners of enterprises.

Legitimate assets and capital of enterprises.

Rights of enterprises:

1. Find markets, customers, and sign contracts proactively.

2. Hire employees to serve the business.

Enterprise manager is the manager of a company who is entitled to enter into the company's transactions on behalf of the company.

Related person means any individual that has a direct relationship with the enterprise, such as the enterprise manager;

Enterprise restructuring means a total or partial division, consolidation, or acquisition of an enterprise.

Export: the act of sending goods or services to another country for sale.

Import: the act of bringing goods or services into a country from abroad for sale.

Rights of enterprises:

a) Find markets, customers, and sign contracts proactively.

b) Engage in export and import.

Enterprise's seal: a special mark that you put on a document, to show that it is legal or official.

Every enterprise is entitled to decide the contents of its seal.

Export-processing zone: a territory where the government allows the import of various products without levying any taxes so that goods can be manufactured and exported from the country.

Industrial park: an area of land developed for the purpose of industrial development.

Economic zone: an area with particular economic advantages in which business and trade laws are different from the rest of the country to encourage investment there.

Development of infrastructure of industrial parks in the economic zone;

Development of housing for workers in economic zones.

Exemption of income tax: the process of freeing someone from paying taxes on a specified amount of income for themselves.

Income tax: a tax levied by a government directly on the income of an individual or a business.

Industrial parks: an area of land zoned and planned for the purpose of industrial development rather than residential or commercial needs.

Export-processing zones: areas within developing countries that offer incentives to promote economic growth by attracting foreign investment.

Hi-tech zone: an industrial district.

Administrative divisions that are given investment incentives:

a) Administrative divisions in extremely disadvantaged areas;

b) Export-processing zones, hi-tech zones, industrial parks, economic zones.

Economic concentration: concentration of companies on the market in order to form larger enterprises.

The merger of enterprises: a combination of two enterprises into one.

The economic concentration includes the following categories:

a) The merger of enterprises;

b) Consolidation of enterprises;

c) Acquisition of enterprises;

d) A joint venture between/among enterprises;

Export and import of goods

Import of goods means the act of bringing of goods into the territory.

Export of goods means the act of bringing of goods out of the territory.

Exclusive customs zones

Temporary export of goods for re-import means the bringing of goods overseas or into special zones in a territory which are regarded as exclusive customs zones according to the provisions of law.

Excessive quantity: too much or too many.

Delivery of goods in excessive quantity.

The purchaser may reject or accept the excessive quantity of goods that the seller delivers.

Existing house or building means any construction (house or building) has been completed and put into operation.

SECTION F:

Founding shareholder means an individual or organization that owns at least an ordinary share and signs in the list of founding shareholders of the joint-stock company.

Founding shareholders of a joint-stock company.

Ordinary shares of founding shareholders.

Founding shareholders must register at least 20% of total authorized ordinary shares on upon business registration.

Founder means someone who establishes or contributes capital to establish an organization.

The founder of an enterprise may sign contracts serving the establishment and operation of the enterprise.

The founder of the enterprise shall submit the application for enterprise registration prescribed by Law.

Foreign organization means any overseas organization that is established under another country's law.

The copy of the Certificate of Business registration must be consularly legalized if shareholders are foreign organizations.

Financial statement: a formal record of the financial activities and state of an organization, person, or other entity.

Obligations of enterprises:

1. Do accounting, make and submit truthful financial statements in a timely manner according to regulations of law on accounting and statistics.

2. Declare, pay taxes and fulfill other financial obligation as prescribed by

law.

The Director/General Director has the obligations to submit annual financial statements to the Board of members;

Financial obligation: an obligation to pay an amount of money to another party.

The company's owner has the rights to:

a) Decide increases to the company's charter capital; transfer part of or all of the company's charter capital to other organizations and/or individuals;

b) Decide the use of profit after the company's tax liability and other financial obligations are fulfilled;

Foreign currencies: the currency of an overseas country.

Investors may transfer foreign currencies to abroad to serve market survey, research, and other investment preparation.

Foreign investor: an individual holding a foreign nationality and making a business investment in a particular country.

Foreign investors making an investment by buying capital contribution, contributing capital, buying shares of business organizations.

Investment projects of foreign investors;

Foreign investors under a business cooperation contract.

The foreign investor's decision to establish an operating office;

The operating office of a foreign investor in a business cooperation contract has its own seal;

Foreign-invested business organization means a business of which members or shareholders are foreign investors.

Foreign arbitration: means an institutional arbitration selected by the parties; and operating in accordance with foreign law.

Fulfillment: the act of doing something that is required to do.

Fulfillment of tax liability.

Fulfillment of conditions for investment incentives.

Fulfillment of financial obligation.

Fulfillment of social insurance obligations;

Fraudulences or deceits: the action of cheating, or deceiving someone.

Committing fraudulences or deceits about volumes of goods;

Franchisor: The company that allows a third party (known as the franchisee) to run a location of their business under their trademark, trade name, and business model.

In conducting business activities, franchisors shall be entitled to supervise and assist franchisees.

Unless otherwise agreed, franchisors shall have the following rights:

1. To receive franchise sums.

2. To organize advertising for the commercial franchise system and the commercial franchise network.

Franchisee: an individual or company who is given or sold a franchise.

Unless otherwise agreed, franchisees shall have the following rights:

1. To request franchisors to provide fully technical assistance related to the commercial franchise system;

2. To request franchisors to equally treat all franchisees in the commercial franchise system.

Unless otherwise agreed, franchisees shall have the following obligations:

1. To pay franchise sums and other amounts under commercial franchise

contracts;

2. To keep secret the franchised business know-how even after the expiration or termination of commercial franchise contracts;

Fairness: the quality of being fair.

Financial statements: a financial statement consists of an accounting balance, a report on business or production results, a cash flow report and an explanation.

Annual financial statements must be an audited by accredited audit organization.

SECTION G:

The General Meeting of Shareholders

Preferred shares may be converted into ordinary shares under the Resolution of the General Meeting of Shareholders.

The General Meeting of Shareholders consists of all shareholders having a voting right.

SECTION H:

Unemployment insurance: a system that makes payments to people who are unemployed through no fault of their own.

Health insurance: a type of insurance coverage that pays for medical and surgical expenses as a result of sickness or injury.

Enterprises shall buy social insurance, unemployment insurance, and health insurance for employees.

The headquarter: the main office of an organization at a specified location.

The address of the enterprise's headquarter.

The Board of Directors shall hold meetings at the company's headquarter or other locations.

SECTION I:

Internal rules and regulations

The Director/General Director has the following rights:

a) Organize the implementation of Resolutions of the Board of Directors;

b) Organize the implementation of business plans and investment plans of the company;

c) Propose organizational structure, internal rules, and regulations of the company;

d) Suggest plans for dividend payments or loss settlement;

Issuing organization means an organization which issues securities to the public.

The issuing organization shall complete the distribution of securities within ninety days after the certificate of a public offering of securities becomes effective.

An issuing organization being a parent company shall submit a consolidated financial statement according to the accounting law.

Investor: a person or organization that invests money into a business or other organization with the expectation of achieving a profit.

Foreign investors

The Certificate of Investment registration of the foreign investors.

Investment: the action of investing money with an aim at achieving a profitable return.

Investors are entitled to make investments in the business lines that are not banned by laws.

The investments in the activities below are banned:

a) Prostitution;

b) Human trafficking; trade in human tissues and body parts;

Income from business investment;

Investments made by foreign-invested business organizations.

Making investments under business cooperation contracts.

The investor's taxable income: the amount of income used to calculate how much tax the investor owes to the government in a given tax year.

International arbitration: a legal process aimed at solving disagreements between companies or individuals in different states without using a court of law.

Investment incentives: Financial and tax incentives such as various grants and loans; reduced tax rates used to attract investment capital to certain activities or particular areas in a country.

Expansion of investment incentives.

The investment license: a permit from a particular country's government so that a 100 % foreign company can carry on occupations in such country.

Any investor granted the investment license or Certificate of investment may keep executing their investment project according to the investment license or Certificate of registration granted.

International purchase and sale of goods

International purchase and sale of goods shall be conducted in form of export, and import.

Intellectual property rights.

The seller must not sell goods infringing upon intellectual property rights.

Infringements of intellectual property rights.

Intermediary activity: acting on behalf of a party in relation to any matter relating to a transaction.

Intermediary activities in commerce.

Commercial intermediary activities mean activities including representation for traders, commercial brokerage, and commercial agency.

Investor means an organization or individual participating in investment on the securities market.

Assurance of legitimate rights and benefits of investors.

Rights and obligations of investors participating in securities investment funds.

Inside information means undisclosed information on a public company or a public fund.

SECTION J:

Joint-stock company: a company in which shares of its are owned by shareholders.

A joint-stock company may have one or multiple legal representatives.

A joint-stock company must have ordinary shares. Holders of ordinary shares are ordinary shareholders.

Joint venture: two or more companies working together for a particular purpose.

A joint venture between/among enterprises;

SECTION L:

Law on employment = labour law: a law relating to the legal rights and responsibilities of working people and the organizations they work for.

Enterprises shall not show discriminatory behaviors or insult employees in the enterprise;

Legal representative: A person who represents the legal affairs of another.

A joint-stock company may have multiple legal representatives.

The court shall appoint a legal representative for the person who has limited legal capacity.

The legal representative of an enterprise

The enterprise's legal representative has the responsibilities to perform the given rights and obligations in a truthful, careful manner to ensure the enterprise's lawful interests;

Liquidation: the process of closing a business and selling everything it owns in order to pay money that it owes.

Procedures for dissolution and asset liquidation.

Loan capital: a sum of money that people borrow to start a business.

Lien: the legal right to keep someone else's property until a debt owed by that person is discharged.

Unless otherwise agreed, the representative shall be entitled to exercise a lien over entrusted assets and documents to secure the payment of remunerations and expenses due.

Legal validity: the state of being legal.

Legal validity of assessment certificates

Lease of goods: a contract by which one party conveys real estate, equipment, or facilities to another for a specified time, usually in return for a specified rent.

Lease purchase agreement means an agreement between an owner and a renter to rent a property for a certain period of time during which the renter shall pay an option fee to the owner and be entitled to use the property.

Any buildings for under a lease-purchase agreement must meet requirements in terms of quality, safety, environmental hygiene and other necessary services for proper use according to utilities, design and agreement specified in the agreement.

Transfer of lease purchase agreement: The transfer of the lease purchase agreement must be made in writing and certified by the lessor.

Lessor = landlord: owner of the leased asset or property who leases or lets a property to another.

Lessee: someone who has possession of a property under a lease.

The lessor may unilaterally terminate performance of building lease agreement if the lessee intentionally cause serious damage to the leased building;

Obligations of the lessor:

1. Pay compensation for damage caused by the lessor.

2. Enable the lessee to assign their lease-purchase agreement;

Lease agreement: a legal contract between a lessor and lessee in which the lessee (user) has to pay the lessor (owner) in order to have the rights to the use of a property for a period of time.

Any party which unilaterally terminates the lease agreement must notify the other party for at least 01 month prior to the termination, unless otherwise agreed.

Rights and obligations of contracting parties in the lease agreement.

Limited liability company: a corporate whereby its members are not personally liable for the company's debts or liabilities.

The list of members of a limited liability company must have the following information:

Full names, addresses, signatures, permanent residence, nationalities, and other information about members.

Charter capital of a multi-member limited liability company is the total value of the capital contribution to the company promised by the members.

SECTION M:

Members of a partnership include capital contributors and general partners.

Members of a partnership must be natural persons.

In general, the members of a partnership have unlimited liability for the acts of the partnership as a whole.

Mandate: to give a person authority to act in a certain way.

Purchase and sale of goods by mandated dealers mean commercial activities whereby the mandatory conducts the purchase and sale of goods in his/her/its own name under terms agreed upon with the mandator and is entitled to receive mandate commission.

Mandate contracts for purchase and sale of goods must be made in writing or in other forms of equivalent legal validity.

Mandatory: compulsory (required by a law or rule).

A mandatory for purchase and sale of goods is a trader dealing in goods which are consistent with the mandated goods and conducting the purchase and sale of goods under terms agreed upon with the mandator.

A mandatory may accept the mandate for purchase and sale of goods from different mandators.

Member fund means a securities investment fund which consists of at most thirty capital-contributing members being legal persons.

A member fund is established by capital-contributing members on the basis of a capital contribution contract and the fund's charter.

Majority shareholder means a shareholder directly or indirectly owns at least 5% of voting stocks of an issuing organization.

A change in the number of stocks owned by a majority shareholder.

SECTION N:

National business registration portal means a website used for collecting data of online business registration nationwide.

The decision on dissolution of the enterprise shall be posted on National Business Registration Portal.

National Enterprise Registration Database means a set of data about business registration nationwide.

The business registration authority shall update the legal status of the branch or representative office on the National Enterprise Registration Database.

SECTION O:

Organization: any type of civil or political association includes a corporation, government, partnership.

Multi-member limited liability company is an enterprise where members are organizations and/or individuals and they are liable for debts and other liabilities of the enterprise up to the value of capital they contribute to the enterprise.

A single-member limited liability company is an enterprise under the ownership of an organization or individual where the company's owner is liable for the company's debts and other liabilities up to the company's charter capital.

Administrative expense

Operating costs

The administrative expense and operating costs of the enterprise;

Operating cost of the Board of members, salaries, benefits, and other remunerations shall be included in the company's administrative expense.

Ordinary shareholders: people who receive their dividends after preference shareholders are paid.

A joint-stock company must have ordinary shares. Holders of ordinary shares are ordinary shareholders.

Every ordinary shareholder is entitled to:

a) Receive dividends at a rate decided by the General Meeting of Shareholders;

b) Has the preemptive right when buying newly-offered shares in proportion to his/her ordinary shares;

Outward investment = oversea investment: money that is invested in foreign countries.

The Certificate of registration of outward investment.

Investors are encouraged to make an outward investment in order to expand the market.

Option contract: An options contract is an agreement between a buyer and seller that gives the buyer (the owner or holder of the option) the right to buy or sell a particular asset on a specified date at an agreed upon price.

Forward contracts and option contracts.

Rights and obligations of parties to option contracts.

Obligations of principals

Unless otherwise agreed, a principal shall have the following obligations:

1. To supply information, documents, necessary means related to goods and services;

2. To pay brokerage remuneration and other reasonable expenses to the broker.

Unless otherwise agreed, principals must pay all reasonable expenses incurred in relation to brokerage to brokers, even where the brokerage does not bring about any results for principals.

Off-the-plan building means any building which is yet to be built and has not been permitted to put into operation.

The off-the-plan building sale, lease or lease-purchase shall comply with regulations of the regulations of the Law.

The transfer of off-the-plan building sale or lease purchase agreement must be made in writing and certified by the investor.

Open-end fund means a public fund whose certificates, which have undergone a public offering, should be bought back at the request of investors.

Investors have the following rights:

a/ To request fund management companies or supervisory banks to buy back open-end fund certificates;

b/ To transfer fund certificates according to charters of securities investment funds;

SECTION P:

Partnership: a legal form of business in which two or more individuals work together as partners and share management and profits.

Application for registration of a partnership.

Assets of a partnership include contributed assets the ownership of which have been transferred to the company by members.

Permanent residence means the address of an individual's permanent residence/ the address of an organization's headquarter.

Any shareholder that changes his/her permanent residence must promptly notify the company to update the shareholder register.

The certificate of the capital contribution must contain the following information:

Full name, permanent residence, nationality, ID/passport number of every partner; types of partners.

The parent company: a company that has a controlling interest, management and operation in another company.

The manager of the parent company.

A company is considered parent company of another company if the former company owns more than 50% of the charter capital or total ordinary shares of the other company;

Financial statements of the parent company.

Post-tax profit = net profit.

Distribution of post-tax profit.

The preemptive right: a privilege that is granted to shareholders so they can buy additional shares in the company prior to shares being made available for purchase by the general public.

When the company's charter capital is increased, each member has the preemptive right to contribute additional capital.

Preferred shares: shares of a joint-stock company with dividends that are given to shareholders before issuing common stock dividends.

Ordinary shares cannot be converted into preferred shares.

Preferred shares include:

A) Voting preference shares;

B) Shares with preferred dividends;

C) Redeemable preferred shares;

Preferred dividends: dividends that are accrued and paid on a company's preferred shares.

Shares with preferred dividends are shares that pay higher dividends than dividends of ordinary shares.

Holders of shares with preferred dividends do not have the voting right.

Public facilities: facilities provided for the benefit of the community at large including streets, airport; rail, subway, bus station, highways, etc.

Public amenities are useful or pleasant facilities, services, resources, conveniences, facilities provided to the general public for their use or enjoyment.

Development of public facilities and amenities for workers in economic zones.

Public-utility products and services means products and services which are essential for the public use or entertainment.

Enterprises that provide public-utility products and services.

Provision of services: the action of providing or supplying something for use.

Agreements on distributing customers, consumption market, sources of supply of goods, provision of services.

Service providers must satisfy all reasonable requests of their customers for changes during the provision of services.

Pre-delivery: occurring prior to the delivery of something.

Pre-delivery examination of goods.

The purchaser: a person who buys something.

The purchaser may receive or reject the goods where the seller delivers goods earlier than the agreed time, unless otherwise agreed upon by the parties.

Pricing by weight.

The goods price is determined according to the weight of the goods.

Place of payment

Where there is no agreement on a specific place of payment, the purchaser must pay to the seller at the seller's place of business, which is identified at the time of entering into the contract;

Purchase and sale of goods by mandated dealers: means commercial activities whereby the mandatory conducts the purchase and sale of goods and is entitled to receive mandate commission.

Publicity: the quality of being public (by the media).

Public offering of securities means the offering of securities for sale by the mass media, including the Internet;

Forms of a public offering of securities include the first-time public offering of securities, additional offering of shares or rights to buy shares to the public, and other forms.

Modification or supplementation of dossiers of registration of public offering of securities.

Effect of registration of public offering of securities.

Prospectus means a printed document or electronic data that provides details about an investment offering for sale to the public.

For the public offering of stocks or bonds, a prospectus must contain signatures of the chairman of the Board of Directors or the Council of Members or the company president.

Public fund means a securities investment fund which conducts a public offering of fund certificates.

The mobilization of the capital of a public fund shall be conducted by the fund management company within ninety days after the certificate of a public offering of fund certificates takes effect.

Securities investment funds include public funds and member funds.

Public funds include open-end funds and closed funds.

Mobilization of capital for the establishment of public funds.

Public company: a company that has issued securities traded freely on a stock exchange.

A public company is a joint-stock company that:

a/ Has already conducted the public offering of its stocks;

b/ Has its stocks listed at the Stock Exchange or the Securities Trading Center;

Public funds: Public funds include open-end funds and closed funds.

SECTION R:

Resolution of internal dispute: the action of solving an internal dispute.

Rules for resolution of the internal dispute.

Reduction: the process of making something smaller or less in amount, degree, or size.

The reduction of corporate income tax

The exemption, reduction of land rents

Repurchasing stakes: the act of buying back stocks, shares, bonds previously sold.

If the company does not repurchase the stake, the member is entitled to transfer his/her stake to another member or a person other than members.

Repurchase of shares at the request of shareholders.

Repurchase of shares under the company's decision.

Repurchased shares or dividends: the action of buying shares or dividends back.

Withdrawal of payment for repurchased shares or dividends.

Representative: someone who does something officially for another person.

Obligations of representative offices:

1. To conduct commercial promotion activities within the scope permitted by this Law.

2. To pay taxes, fees and charges, and fulfill other financial obligations provided for by law.

Foreign traders are entitled to set up their representative offices or branches in another country.

Pay remunerations and other reasonable expenses to the representative;

Receipt of goods

The lessor shall give the lessee a reasonable time after the receipt of goods for inspection thereof.

Remuneration: payment for work or services.

The representative shall be entitled to remunerations for any contract which is concluded within the contractual scope of representation.

Unless otherwise agreed by the parties, agents shall have the following right:

To enjoy remunerations and other lawful rights and interests brought about by agency activities.

Representation: acting on behalf of someone.

Representation for traders is defined as an arrangement where a trader is granted authorization (hereinafter referred to as the representative) by another trader (hereinafter referred to as the principal) to perform trades under the name or direction of the former, and earn remunerations for his/her representation service rendered.

Duration of representation shall be agreed upon by contracting parties.

Rejection of goods: the act of refusing to accept, or use something.

Rectification: correction

Rectification or replacement of leased goods inappropriate to contracts

Resolution: the action of solving a dispute or problem.

Resolution of commercial disputes.

Real estate trading: means capital investment in building, purchasing, and receiving real estate for sale, for lease, for sublease, for transfer, or for lease purchase;

The real estate trading must be conducted honestly, publicly and transparently.

Prohibited acts:

1. Fraud and deception in real estate trading.

2. Collection of charges, fees and money amounts related to real estate trading in contravention of the provisions of law.

Real estate brokerage means acts as an intermediary between parties in a real estate sale, lease, sublease, transfer, or lease-purchase transactions.

The real estate brokerage remunerations shall be agreed by contracting parties regardless of brokerage transfer price.

Real estate management: the operation, control, and oversight of real estate.

Real estate management service agreement.

Any organizations or individuals who wish to provide real estate management services must establish the enterprise.

Content, time and scope of real estate management, rights and obligations of contracting parties and real estate management price shall be agreed by the contracting parties.

Real estate trading floors mean places where real estate sale, lease, sublease, or transfer are carried out.

An enterprise conducting real estate trading shall take responsibility for disclosure of real estate on the real estate trading floors regarding real estate trading through trading floors.

The manager of real estate trading floors must obtain a broker license.

Real estate counseling means the act of providing advice that significantly affects real estate decisions.

Real estate counseling service agreement.

Real estate transactions: the process whereby rights of real estate is transferred between two or more parties.

The payment for real estate transactions shall be agreed by contracting parties and followed the regulations of laws on payment.

Any real estate service provider is not entitled to be both a broker and a contracting party in a real estate transaction.

To re-export: to export again.

To re-import: to import something back into the country.

Temporary import for re-export of goods.

Temporary export for re-import of goods.

SECTION S:

Sole proprietorships: a business that is owned and operated by one individual.

Sole proprietorships must not issue any kind of shares.

The owner of a sole proprietorship must not concurrently be a household business owner or partner of a partnership.

Each individual may establish only one sole proprietorship.

Shareholder: any person, company, or institution that owns at least a share of a joint-stock company.

The General Meeting of Shareholders.

A list of shareholders being foreign investors.

Copies of the ID card of shareholders being individuals;

If shareholders are foreign organizations, the copy of the Certificate of Business registration must be consularly legalized.

State-owned company means any enterprise of which 100% charter capital is held by the State and undertakes commercial activities on behalf of the state.

State-owned company shall be organized and administered in accordance with the law on enterprises.

Subsidiary: a company that is owned or controlled by a holding company.

The parent company shall be responsible for any damage to the subsidiary.

Depending on the type of business of the subsidiary, the parent company shall perform its rights and obligations as a member/partner, owner, or shareholder of the subsidiary.

Stake means an interest, an amount of money or assets that a member/partner invests or promises to invest in a business or venture.

The stake shall be split equally among the representatives if the owner, or shareholder fails to determine the stake of each authorized representative.

Social insurance: a form of compensation provided by a government for the elderly, the disabled, or the unemployed.

The enterprise's debts shall be paid in the following order:

a) Unpaid salaries, severance pay, social insurance as prescribed by law, other benefits of employees according to collective bargaining agreement and signed employment contracts;

b) Tax debts;

c) Other debts.

Securities issuance: the act of issuing stocks, shares, bonds.

Stake: the part of a business that someone owns since he has invested money in it

Every organization and individual is entitled to buy shares in joint-stock companies.

Each member in a joint-stock company is entitled to give part or all of their stake to another person.

Share certificate = certificate of stock: a legal document that certifies ownership of a specific number of stock or shares in a corporation.

If there is a mistake in the contents and format of the share certificates issued by the company, the rights and interests of their holders shall not be affected.

In case a share certificate is lost, damaged, or otherwise destroyed, the shareholder shall be reissued with another share certificate at the shareholder's request.

Securities investment funds: funds established from capital contributions of investors in order to make a profit from securities investment.

Trading in valuable papers, securities, or making investments via securities investment funds;

Sale and purchase of goods: commercial activities whereby the seller is obliged to deliver and transfer the ownership of goods to the purchaser and receive the payment.

Contracts for sale and purchase of goods may be expressed in written form or verbal.

Purchase and sale of goods by mandated dealers.

The seller: a person who sells something.

The seller may be liable for any defects of goods that are already examined by the purchaser.

The seller must assure that:

1. The goods are lawful;

2. The ownership right of the purchaser over goods sold is not disputed by any third party;

Suspension of payment for goods: the act of stopping (doing) something for a period of time.

The purchaser who has proofs of deceit of the seller shall have the right to suspend the payment for goods.

Service provider: a company that provides a service.

The service provider has obligation to provide a service to another party and has the right to receive payment;

Rights and obligations of commercial advertising service providers.

Sale promotion: Sales promotion covers marketing activities like advertising.

Provision of sale promotion service.

Conduct sale promotion for goods and/or services.

Sale promotion goods and services must be traded lawfully.

Obligations of traders conducting sale promotion.

Sub-lease: a contract that allows a person to rent a house, flat or office from someone who is renting it from someone else.

Lessees shall be entitled to sub-lease goods only when they obtain consents of lessors.

Lessees shall be responsible for sub-leased goods, unless they otherwise agree with lessors.

Sublease agreement: a legally binding contract made between a lessor and a lessee, with the landlord's consent.

Rights and obligations of contracting parties in the sublease agreement.

Securities: stocks, bonds, fund certificates;

Bond means a type of securities certifying their holders' legitimate rights and benefits to a portion of liabilities of an issuing organization.

Stock means a type of securities certifying their holders' legitimate rights and benefits to a portion of the equity of an issuing organization.

Fund certificate means a type of securities certifying investors' ownership over a portion of the contributed capital of a public fund.

Investors have the following obligations:

a/ To abide by decisions of the investors' congress;

b/ To pay in full money amounts for purchase of fund certificates;

Securities trading market means a place where buy and sell orders are rallied and securities transactions are conducted.

A securities trading center shall organize a securities trading market for securities of issuing organizations unqualified for listing at a stock exchange.

A trading member has the following rights:

a/ To use the trading system and services provided by the stock exchange or the securities trading center;

b/ To receive information on securities trading market from the stock exchange or securities trading center;

Securities business means the performance of such professional operations as securities dealing, securities brokerage, securities investment consultancy, securities investment fund management.

A securities company or a fund management company has its establishment and operation license revoked in the following case:

It fails to commence its securities business operation within twelve months after being granted the establishment and operation license;

Securities brokerage means an operation of a securities company acting as an intermediary to buy or sell securities on behalf of its clients.

For a securities company, the conditions for registration of securities depository activities include:

a/ Having a license for establishment and performance of securities brokerage or dealing operation;

b/ Having a place, facilities and equipment in service of securities registration and depository and securities transaction payment activities.

Securities dealing means buying or selling securities by a securities company for itself.

Securities companies may conduct the securities issuance underwriting operation only when they conduct the securities dealing operation.

Securities depository means the receipt of securities for deposit, preservation or transfer to customers.

Time limit for grant of securities depository registration certificates.

Suspension or revocation of securities depository registration certificates.

Organization and operation of securities depository centers.

Securities registration means the acknowledgment of ownership right and other rights of a securities owner.

For a securities company, the conditions for registration of securities depository activities include:

a/ Having a license for establishment and performance of securities brokerage or dealing operation;

b/ Having a place, facilities and equipment in service of securities registration and depository and securities transaction payment activities.

Securities portfolio management means the management by a securities fund management company of the securities owned by an investor.

Securities investment fund means a fund formed from investors' contributed capital for the purpose of earning profits from the securities investment.

A supervision contract between the supervisory bank and the securities investment fund management company;

Securities companies and securities investment fund management companies shall be organized in the form of limited liability companies or joint-stock companies in accordance with the Enterprise Law.

Securities trading centers

Stock exchanges and securities trading centers have the function of organizing and supervising the trading of securities listed at such stock exchanges and securities trading centers.

Securities depository centers

Operation of securities depository centers shall comply with the provisions of the Law and their charters.

Securities practitioners

When working for securities companies, securities practitioners are entitled to open securities trading accounts for themselves at the very securities companies.

Securities trading accounts

Securities practitioners may not use money and securities on customers' accounts without being entrusted by such customers.

Securities investment funds: securities investment funds include public funds and member funds.

SECTION T:

The company's charter: a document that regulates a company's external activities.

The quantity, rights and obligations of the legal representative of the enterprise shall be specified in the company's charter.

Obligations of member:

1. Comply with the company's charter.

2. Comply with resolutions and decisions of the Board of members.

Trader: a person whose business is buying and selling goods, currency, or stocks.

In commercial activities, traders of all economic sectors are protected and equal before the law.

Traders must be responsible for the quality and lawfulness of goods or services they trade in or provide.

Technical secrets

Shares, bonds of a joint-stock company may be purchased with convertible foreign currencies, gold, land use right value, the value of intellectual property rights, technologies, technical secrets, and other assets prescribed by the company's charter.

The enterprise's proper name: a name used for an organization, spelled with initial capital letters, e.g.,

Undue debt: a debt that you are not yet required to pay.

Payment of undue debts.

Transferring stakes: the act of conveying stocks, shares, bonds from one person to another.

Contributing partners are entitled to:

Transfer their stakes to other persons;

Telecommunications service: any public service corporation that has traditionally provided telephone and similar services.

Network infrastructure: an interconnected group of computer systems that allow devices to connect and communicate.

Telecommunications services with network infrastructure.

Projects of investment of foreign investors in sea transport, provision of telecommunications services with network infrastructure; afforestation, publishing, and journalism.

The transportation of goods = the handover of the goods

Goods sellers shall bear the expenses for transportation of goods to the agreed places;

The transportation of goods in transit.

The examination of goods: the act or process of testing/examining goods.

Where the purchaser or the purchaser's representative does not conduct the examination of goods before the delivery of goods as agreed, the seller may deliver the goods according to the contract.

Transit of goods: the carrying of goods from one place to another.

Transit service contracts.

Transit service contracts must be made in writing.

Time of transferring ownership of goods

Ownership of goods shall be passed from the seller to the purchaser as from the time of handover of the goods.

Trade fair: trade show, trade exhibition.

Trade fairs and exhibitions: an event at which objects such as paintings, works of art or other items are shown to the public.

Representative offices of traders shall not be allowed to directly organize or participate in trade fairs and exhibitions.

Transparency: the condition of being transparent (honesty and openness).

Principles of securities activities and securities market operation:

1. Fairness, publicity and transparency.

2. Protection of legitimate rights and benefits of investors.

3. Compliance with law.

SECTION U:

Unilateral termination: (of a termination) performed by only one party without the agreement of another or the others.

Unilateral termination of the lease agreement.

Urgent measures

The application of urgent measures shall comply with the provisions of law.

Unreasonable costs: costs that are not reasonable.

When the seller causes disadvantages or unreasonable costs to the purchaser, the purchaser shall have the right to request the seller to deal with such disadvantages or bear such costs.

SECTION V:

Voting capital means the stake or shares under the ownership of a person, corporation, or partnership who has the right to vote in the election of the board of directors.

Foreign investors' holding means the total holding of the voting capital of all foreign investors in a company.

Valuable papers: A special type of property.

Property comprises valuable papers, objects, money, and property rights.

SECTION W:

Warranty: a company's written promise to replace or repair a product that you buy from them for a specific period of time.

Goods are purchased and sold under warranty.

Unless otherwise agreed, the seller must bear all warranty expenses.

CONCLUSION

Thank you again for downloading this book on *"Legal Terminology And Phrases: Master 350+ Essential Business, Enterprise, Commercial and Investment Terms And Phrases Explained With Examples In 10 Minutes A Day."* and reading all the way to the end. I'm extremely grateful.

If you know of anyone else who may benefit from the essential *Business, Enterprise, Commercial and Investment* terms and phrases explained with examples that are revealed in this book, please help me inform them of this book. I would greatly appreciate it.

Finally, if you enjoyed this book and feel that it has added value to your work and study in any way, please take a couple of minutes to share your thoughts and post a REVIEW on Amazon. Your feedback will help me to continue to write other books of IELTS topic that helps you get the best results. Furthermore, if you write a simple REVIEW with positive words for this book on Amazon, you can help hundreds or perhaps thousands of other readers who may want to improve their legal vocabulary so that they could get the greatest achievements in work and study. Like you, they worked hard for every penny they spend on books. With the information and recommendation you provide, they would be more likely to take action right away. We really look forward to reading your review.

Thanks again for your support and good luck!

If you enjoy my book, please write a POSITIVE REVIEW on Amazon.

-- Dr. Peter Johnson --

CHECK OUT OTHER BOOKS

Go here to check out other related books that might interest you:

Ielts Academic Vocabulary: Master 3000+ Academic Vocabularies By Topics Explained In 10 Minutes A Day.

https://www.amazon.com/dp/B07F3X3GJ8

IELTS Listening Strategies: The Ultimate Guide with Tips, Tricks and Practice on How to Get a Target Band Score of 8.0+ in 10 Minutes a Day.

https://www.amazon.com/dp/B07845S1MG

IELTS Reading Strategies: The Ultimate Guide with Tips and Tricks on How to Get a Target Band Score of 8.0+ in 10 Minutes a Day.

https://www.amazon.com/dp/B077TWDSJJ

Ielts Writing Task 2 Samples : Over 450 High-Quality Model Essays for Your Reference to Gain a High Band Score 8.0+ In 1 Week (Box set) https://www.amazon.com/dp/B077BYQLPG

Ielts Academic Writing Task 1 Samples: Over 450 High Quality Samples for Your Reference to Gain a High Band Score 8.0+ In 1 Week (Box set) https://www.amazon.com/dp/B077CC5ZG4

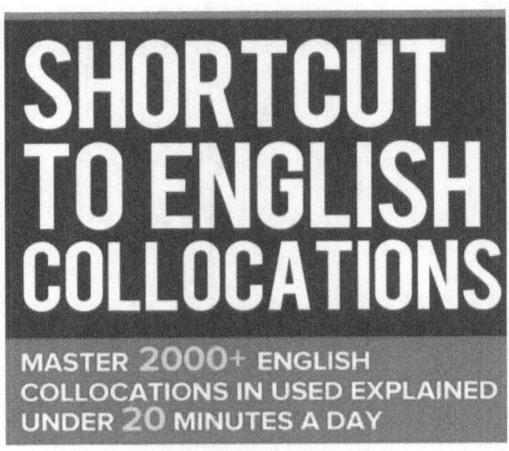

Shortcut To English Collocations: Master 2000+ English Collocations In Used Explained Under 20 Minutes A Day (5 books in 1 Box set)

https://www.amazon.com/dp/B06W2P6S22

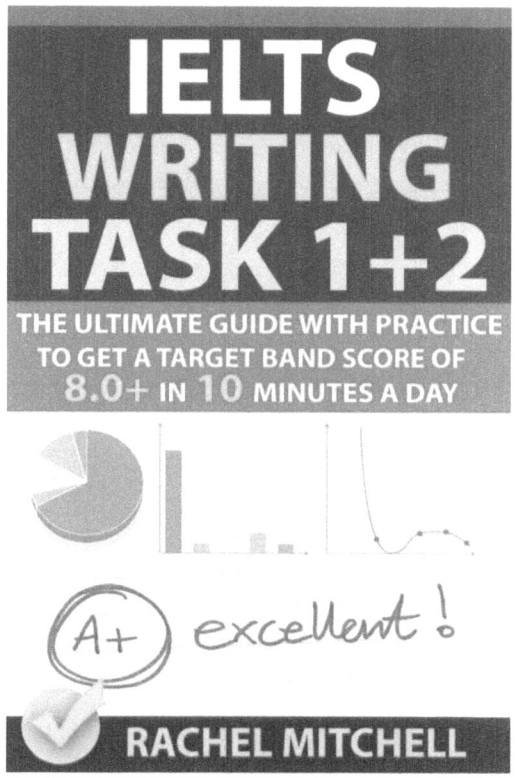

IELTS Writing Task 1 + 2: The Ultimate Guide with Practice to Get a Target Band Score of 8.0+ In 10 Minutes a Day

https://www.amazon.com/dp/B075DFYPG6

IELTS Speaking Strategies: The Ultimate Guide With Tips, Tricks, And Practice On How To Get A Target Band Score Of 8.0+ In 10 Minutes A Day.

https://www.amazon.com/dp/B075JCW65G

Shortcut To Ielts Writing: The Ultimate Guide To Immediately Increase Your Ielts Writing Scores.

https://www.amazon.com/dp/B01JV7EQGG

Common English Mistakes Explained With Examples: Over 600 Mistakes Almost Students Make and How to Avoid Them in Less Than 5 Minutes A Day

https://www.amazon.com/dp/B072PXVHNZ

Paraphrasing Strategies: 10 Simple Techniques For Effective Paraphrasing In 5 Minutes Or Less

https://www.amazon.com/dp/B071DFG27Q

Legal Vocabulary In Use: Master 600+ Essential Legal Terms And Phrases Explained In 10 Minutes A Day

http://www.amazon.com/dp/B01L0FKXPU

Legal Terminology And Phrases: Essential Legal Terms Explained You Need To Know About Crimes, Penalty And Criminal Procedure

http://www.amazon.com/dp/B01L5EB54Y

Civil Law Vocabulary In Use: Master 350+ Essential Civil Law Terms And Phrases Explained With Examples In 10 Minutes A Day

https://www.amazon.com/dp/B0781TQWGV

Criminal Law Vocabulary In Use: Master 400+ Essential Criminal Law Terms And Phrases Explained With Examples In 10 Minutes A Day https://www.amazon.com/dp/B078KLR51Z

www.ingramcontent.com/pod-product-compliance
Lightning Source LLC
Chambersburg PA
CBHW030445220526
45464CB00006B/2424